About the Author

My younger days were spent in rural Australia in the 1950s. Country life created an inquiring mind; as a result of having time on my own, I developed a connection with the spirit world, although I am not at all religious. I have had many unusual and beautiful experiences in my life; it has brought me very close to nature. As a result, I am always thinking out of the box. What if. Why. These where questions I pestered my mother with. I have done this all my life, questioned everything.

Out of the Box Thinking

Geoff Parton

Out of the Box Thinking

Olympia Publishers
London

www.olympiapublishers.com
OLYMPIA PAPERBACK EDITION

Copyright © Geoff Parton 2022

The right of Geoff Parton to be identified as author of
this work has been asserted in accordance with sections 77 and 78 of
the Copyright, Designs and Patents Act 1988.

All Rights Reserved

No reproduction, copy or transmission of this publication
may be made without written permission.
No paragraph of this publication may be reproduced,
copied or transmitted save with the written permission of the publisher,
or in accordance with the provisions
of the Copyright Act 1956 (as amended).

Any person who commits any unauthorised act in relation to
this publication may be liable to criminal
prosecution and civil claims for damage.

A CIP catalogue record for this title is
available from the British Library.

ISBN: 978-1-80074-455-4

First Published in 2022

Olympia Publishers
Tallis House
2 Tallis Street
London
EC4Y 0AB

Printed in Great Britain

Acknowledgements

I would like to thank my wife Jayne for listening and giving me pointers where needed. Her opinion of life is very similar to mine.

Chapter 1

In this book I will try to explain several different possibilities covering the meaning of life, where we come from and where we are going to. I'm also going to try and explain what I think is really happening with this thing we call time.

I suppose the first and most obvious explanation is that everything is just as we see it — an atheist would go along with this theory. Unfortunately, there are a lot of atheists in the world who are unable to see any spiritual outcome in their lives. As a result, they become go-getters for material gain and wealth, because to them, that's all there is.

This way of belief indicates that this world is meandering along an unknown path or direction, and as such, anything can happen and will happen along the way. It leaves no room for any advancement other than material advancement. This way of thinking does not explain certain things that happen in one's life, such as any unusual psychic events.

There is no room with this way of thinking to explain

the unexplained, other than to use words like chance, or coincidence or luck etc. Everything is explained from a material viewpoint, and the unexplained is simply written off as unexplainable. That's all there is in this theory!

This theory, and I call it a theory for obvious reasons which will become apparent later in the book, comes from — in my opinion — a closed-minded outlook. When I say closed-minded, I don't say that with any disrespect, but it seems that the theory of when you're dead you're dead, is too simple, and the meaning of life would then have no substance; as a result, it would leave me, and most other people empty. The viewpoint that everything just is as we see it, is not only closed-minded, but also leaves no room for any spiritual development, or any unknowns to be explored.

To think that before we are born, we don't exist, and after we die, we also cease to exist, is in my mind bizarre! This is a materialistic thought, where only material things exist. Well, I ask you this, what would be the point of it all?

Most people have been, and are still swayed by, some type of religion, a way or direction for someone to follow, etc. Most people are followers, leaving a minority to do the leading — whether it be religious leaders or leaders in government. It seems to me that the people that are leading, end up realising that there are material advantages in their positions; as a result, very few have a strong spiritual sense. Material advantages for leaders tend to steer their decision making in a certain direction, a material direction; as a result, it has a major influence on the rest of the population who are forced to go along with those decisions.

This is one of the biggest problems we have as a

society; our leaders are not the type of people we should have at the helm, as we all know that their agenda is almost all ways misguided, as is with anyone in control.

Whether we realise it or not, we are spiritual beings enjoying a life of experiences. Firstly, before being born — when we are still in the spirit world, we choose to be born into a semi- pre-written world; when I say pre-written, I mean it has a basic blueprint with perimeters, enabling us to experience anything in life we choose as we go along. In saying that, I mean we have what is commonly called instinct, or the blueprint of life. For example, we all have built-in abilities to walk, run, listen, talk, and eat etc. But there are untold limitations for example, we can't fly or be in two places at once.

This theory leaves open the opportunity for us to make decisions which affect outcomes, and hence the whole of what we call the future is being written by us within those blueprinted borders. This being the case, what may or may not happen is totally down to our decision making. In this theory the future has not happened, and is still open to being made by us, without going outside the limitations that are pre-inbuilt.

This most probably would rule out any chance of time travel into the future, as the future would not have happened yet. It also means that we are guardians of our own destiny, and as such we will, and must be very careful of our decision making, as we are responsible for the future. The idea that we are here making our own destiny by the decisions we make, means we are here to experience and learn, like a school of sorts.

I assume that there are more spiritual beings on the

planet than not. Taking that into account, we need to change our ways, i.e., our choice of leaders, and then our general attitude towards each other. We must not be bolshy with the theory that, if I think I'm correct and you don't agree, **you** must be incorrect, which as we know can lead to insane wars.

I think that most of the population would go along with this theory that we are in control of our destiny; that being said, why don't we do something about improving our current situation? Or are we so tied up with work and sports etc. that it becomes just too hard, and we leave it to someone else, or perhaps the invisible man, ha, ha!

Chapter 2

Another possibility, which is similar to the last one. However, the big difference being that although we are here to experience, we assume we have choices. The choices we think we are making have already been pre-planned. Every choice you think you just made was going to happen anyway, making it possible for the great book of life, as I call it, to have already been written, or should we really call it — 'The Great Play of Life'.

This great book of life in a sense, isn't really life but simply a stage where part of the spirit world can experience anything. The point is, that with our lack of understanding, our five senses make us think and feel that everything is real. It's a bit like reading a fiction story book, we know it's not real, but the story is so good that it seems real.

Imagine that you have become a character in this fiction book that you are reading, then imagine your memory of everything else outside in a way, has been wiped; you would feel if you didn't know anything better, that the book that you are reading is in fact your real world! You would become as one in the story because you would have nothing else to compare it with.

This is the very reason why when we arrive here in the form of a baby, that we have no recollection whatsoever where we came from, or our 'real' world. The whole play here is designed that way, otherwise we would not get the full impact and understanding of the experiences that we are experiencing. In some cases, we would probably leave early if some problems seemed too hard to handle.

This being the case, we are all under an illusion. The illusion is that we think we have free choice and the ability to make decisions, when in fact, we are here to experience peculiar things that don't exist in the spirit world — emotions being at the top of the list.

We choose a lifestyle of experiences to get the understanding we want and need, for our spirit or soul to grow or expand. This choice is made in the spirit realm before we arrive here. This means that the life we have chosen will suit our needs, therefore adding credence that the stage play has already been written.

The choices we think we are making, are just here to make this play seem more real. After all, we are here to experience, in order to grasp understanding of physical feelings and emotions and how we handle them; these are on the top of the list in my opinion.

Chapter 3

Just imagine that there is no time, and all this is an illusion; everything just is NOW! This thing we call time makes us think that there is a past and therefore a future. To say there is no time may sound a bit weird, so it is possible that we are, and have been, completely hoodwinked into believing that all there is, is what we have here now.

This thing called time: future, past and present, doesn't allow us to go back or forward in this stage play.

Let's face it, we can't go back in time because it has become the past, which is now just a memory. So, if the past becomes something that does not exist — what we call the future also does not exist because it hasn't happened, and so becomes hearsay, or a probable possibility.

The world as we know it is made up of minuscule to larger, to very large particles, they all spin and revolve around other particles.

When I was a young boy, an atom was considered the smallest thing known to man, now scientists know that there are many other smaller bodies like quarks, neutrinos, bosons etc. that are smaller than atoms, and now even smaller things that presently scientists are not able to measure yet. They come from {what they call} 'string' theory — to get a grip on their size, it would be like this… If a single atom was blown up to be the size of our solar system, a string from the string theory would be the size of a tree.

Take our body for instance, if you were to magnify any part of our body, any part at all, you would find that we are not really solid. We are a conglomerate of tiny particles spinning around other particles with space in between — as is everything we know in the physical world. If a human were expanded to the size of the universe, a plane would easily be able to fly through us; in fact, from an ant's point of view, we would probably appear as a universe.

That being so, you may ask why we are in a certain shape? Well, we are 'held' in a physical shape of sorts — in our case it's the human shape, because our spiritual energy being has chosen to take a human form.

I will go into that later, but for the moment there is nothing that is solid, we only think it's solid because of our size in comparison relative to the tiny particles that we are made up of. It appears that we are solid simply because we can't see the tiny particles that are so small spinning around each other in our individual space, so we feel and appear solid.

If you look at anything whether it be a planet, a star, a motorcar, a human or a dog, we are all masses of tiny particles spinning around each other, that have taken a particular shape for a particular reason. This is where the spiritual world comes into play.

To understand why a dog looks like a dog, and why a human looks like a human, we have to understand that these are just parts of the greater energy of the spirit world, or whatever name you may want to call it. When this great spiritual energy desires to experience something, whether it be a leaf, a dog, a horse, or a human, it makes no difference. It enters a material reflection of itself, made up of those tiny atoms and quarks etc. we see — which I was just talking about. This being so, it is quite easy to realise that this material world that we feel we are living in, is only a temporary place.

This explains the reason for what we call birth and death; one has to step onto the stage, play their part and then leave the stage.

Chapter 4

As you know, when the spirit leaves a body, whether it be a tree or a human, what is left is simply a conglomerate of tiny revolving atoms and quarks, etc. Without the driver/spirit, that conglomerate starts to fall apart, as there is nothing to hold it together any more.

In a physical sense, we are individuals, but we are only individuals in the physical world.

Be it planets, stars, cars, dogs, horses, trees, it makes no difference, the physical world is only a reflection of the spiritual world, which is the real world.

There is nothing solid, everything is just small or large things spinning around each other; micro-dots if you like. Everything is a reflection of the power of the oneness in the spirit world; when I say spirit world, I mean the energy force that is all, and controls all.

There can be, and there are, many names for this dimension, spirit world, God, supreme energy, it is everything, all it has created is a reflection of itself we call the physical world.

So, while what we see around us appears to be real and

solid, it is only temporary, and therefore disposable in a sense. At a glance, from our perspective, but as I just said, everything is made in an image of this great energy, oneness, spirit, or God as most people seem to refer to this phenomenon.

Unfortunately, most people think God is an individual sitting up there on a throne with a long white beard or something similar. This is not the way it is the oneness or spirit energy is complete and is in all and everything, making the spirit world, the real world — we are all part of it. This material world we exist in at the moment is only a temporary stage play if you like. When your part in the play is over, you leave the stage.

Removing the spirit from the body, which we call dying, is like taking the driver out of the car; the body collapses as it has no driver, or no life in operation, unless it has the spiritual driver. All life forms that are on our planet and all other planets, galaxies and universes, need a driving force, as they are also alive because they have movement. A driver is needed on any level, to create their movement, or their ability to sustain life on any of them.

It is always amusing to me that we still use the word death or dying, because they are totally incorrect. The spirit world continues always, and since we are of the spirit world, we also continue always.

The only thing that dies is the body we leave behind, and even that in a sense does not die, it only transforms into something else, albeit dust or dirt.

Chapter 5

To get your head around this type of thinking, you have to throw away lots of pre-conceived ideas. One of the biggest problems that we have as humans, is that we have been given an understanding that we are separate and therefore individual, so according to our makeup, we feel, or may feel, important! This feeling of being important can and does often get out of hand — we call it ego.

The problem is that our ego often gets us into trouble because most humans have no understanding that they are just a physical mirror image if you like, of the spiritual self, which is totally one.

Individuality and ego go well together it seems, they make us come up with different viewpoints of life and how we should live it... for example, different religions and different ideas on what is best, arise from individuality. And then ego comes along and tries to push its point across, creating disharmony and confusion, often ending up in wars.

This sense of individualism goes against what is real,

and therefore often encourages us to go in the wrong direction. We can stay divided because of this individual feeling.

If everybody on the planet was on the same 'track', and everybody got along with each other, there would be no war or any of these other emotions that often create a negative view point. As a result, the human race would advance spiritually quite rapidly. As I said, this is our greatest handicap thinking that we are individuals rather than not realising that we are in fact, one.

Chapter 6

Try to imagine for a moment that there is no such thing as time. From your perspective, this might seem a bizarre thing to say or even think, but I'm going to explain what I think is really happening with this thing we call time…

When we talk about time, we are also talking about distance and speed, because you can't have any one of those things without the other. Distance and speed equal time in a sense.

For example, if you were in one spot and you could see and touch all or everything at the same moment, you would find that it takes no time because there would be no distance and everything would be in a way, simultaneously happening.

I want you to ponder on that for a moment. Currently, if we want to get from one point to another point, in the shortest period of what we call time, we will endeavour to go faster, correct? If we could reach the speed of light with our latest spacecraft, we would then be able to get from one point being earth for example, to another planet fairly quickly, but even then, the universe is so vast that it would take many light years to get to some of these planets physically.

So, the theory of going at light speed, is still not very fast in the **big** picture, since light itself is not instant but is presumed travelling at a certain speed.

Some of the light from distant stars that scientists have discovered, they say reaches us when the star itself has already died out and vanished. This means if we had been travelling to that star at the speed of light, it wouldn't be there when we arrived! Somewhere along the journey the light would just disappear.

From a micro-point of view to the largest macro viewpoint, everything is orbiting something else. Take the atom and the quark spinning around each other, and now take the largest heavenly bodies, universes orbiting other universes, we then get a better picture of what is happening to everything from atoms to universes. It's happening within our own bodies also, tiny little things spinning around other tiny little things.

So, what is big and what is small, that all depends on our viewpoint. For example, a man walks into the room who is say one hundred and ninety centimetres tall, we think, 'wow that's a tall man,' until the next man comes into the room who is two hundred and five centimetres tall, so what happens to the one hundred- and ninety-centimetres tall man? He then becomes small in comparison.

When we stand still, we think we are effectively stopped; this of course is completely incorrect, because the heavenly body in this case, the earth, is not stationary, it is in fact, spinning around many thousands of miles an hour, not to mention that the galaxy that we exist in, is also spinning around other galaxies at the same time at some amazing speed, of which the scientists have no idea. These galaxies are also in a universe, that's spinning along with many other universes.

It's like when you stir up a bucket of water with little flecks of silver in it, you stir and stir until it's rotating at a great speed, then you take a close look at it and realise, there is no beginning or end.

Consider for a moment that, that is space, and all those little specs are in fact planets and stars, there would be no beginning or end as it would all be just swirling around.

In order to calculate speed, we first of all have to compare it with something else that is either going at a lesser or a greater speed. It's a little bit like size, in order to recognise the big man, we have to see the smaller man first, it's only then that we can make a comparison.

We can be either or both at the same time, it's all a matter of our viewpoint.

So, getting back to speed, if when we think we are going fast, this can only be determined by looking at something that is not going as fast. In other words, speed and size can only be determined by a comparison.

When we are on an airplane, the feeling is — while sitting and watching a movie, that we are in fact stationary. But of course, as we all know, the aircraft is flying at roughly one thousand kilometres an hour, so when we're sitting in our seats, we are not stationary at all.

In order to get to the front of the aircraft, we have to get out of our seat and walk forward; we are not travelling at walking pace, but we are travelling at one thousand kilometres an hour, plus our walking speed of about three kilometres an hour. If no one told us the aircraft was moving, we would think that we are only travelling at walking speed.

So, back on the aircraft travelling at the one thousand kilometres an hour… the landmass we are comparing our speed with, isn't stationary either — it is also travelling at an incredible speed; the earth is moving around in our solar system at an unknown speed.

So, what does this tell us? Well, it tells me that we have no real idea of just how fast we are going. It's all relative!

Therefore, it's impossible to gauge the speed of something, unless you can compare it with something else that is going slower or faster. True speed can only be determined from the time it takes to go from a true stationary place to another true stationary place, it's then you can work out the speed and hence… time.

It therefore becomes apparent that it is quite impossible to say just how fast this planet and the galaxy, and even this universe, is moving, unless you could compare it with something else that was totally stationary, but wait a moment, there is nothing that is totally stationary!

Again, it's all relative. This being so, time, as we know it, is incorrect, so time becomes relative also.

Chapter 7

We have established here, that everything is rotating around another body.

So, what we are seeing is that every time we make a discovery of some sort, we realise that size really doesn't mean a lot, because it is continually changing. There's no accuracy in the description large or small, it's all just a comparison with something else, hence our concept of time is also changing to fit into our known belief. Who knows, one day they may discover that on some of these tiny particles that spin around other tiny particles, there could even be life of some sort, just because we don't have any understanding now of what is large and what is small. At the other end of the scale, who knows all these universes may be a singularity in itself! Anything and everything are possible… There are untold amounts of unknown unknowns.

Our so-called knowledge today is simply based on our limited discoveries, so what is correct today, tomorrow may be completely incorrect. As I said, everything is cyclical, spinning around something else; as a result, it's not really going anywhere other than in a type of vortex. That said, everything is all-ready, so it's quite clear to me, that we are here to experience what is, rather than to change or direct what might be.

In the old days when we started measuring things, we had to have a common denominator. In the UK, the King put his foot forward and said, "We will call the length of my foot — a foot!" And so, the English measurement was calculated all from the King's foot. Of course, this wasn't very accurate, but it was a starting point for some type of measuring.

My point is that the divisions we divide things into, were and are, totally man-made.

Take temperature for example, when we say it's hot or cold, we use a starting point which is called zero, that zero point was taken from a decision that was made when water turns to ice.

In other words, it is totally man-made, and in fact true zero is -273.1 centigrade, which again has been determined by a man-made starting point. In this case, scientists believe that atoms would stop moving at -273.1 centigrade.

By now, we're starting to see that there is no beginning and no end as everything is cyclical, and always is from the perspective of God/source, or spirit world.

With that in mind, we have established that everything is revolving around and around as in a bucket of a swirling water.

There is a centre, and if you were to imagine that you are in the centre, everything else would be swirling around you — all stars, all galaxies, and everything that is on these planets. From your perspective, you would be able to see everything in your universe at the same time, because it would be all around you. Therefore, from your standing point there would be no need for any such thing as time because everything would be visible to you at once. This idea indicates that everything IS already — there is no future or past, as it all IS, at the same time. This means that the whole book of life has been written and we are just experiencing a segment of it.

Getting back to time, let's take a look at true stationary or a stopped position, in other words, when we stop as I said before, we are only stopping on a body that is moving, such as if you stopped walking on the airplane and decided to sit down, then you may consider you are stopped, but we all know that you are not stopped because the plane is moving. It's the same on this planet in everyday life… When we stop, we think we have actually stopped, but that's not true, we are only stopped on a moving body because the planet is still moving, so when we are stopped we're not stopped at all.

We have established that measuring temperature and size, are both man-made as far as the measurement goes; in saying that, we can now assume that those measurements are designed for us and by us, which means that they are designed to fit into our world, and our way of thinking, therefore are only relevant to us.

I suppose you can guess where I'm going with this — the creator, or God, or the energy/intelligence/sentient consciousness — whatever you like to call it, is able to be, and see all at once.

Now, imagine that this energy field is like an enormous

bubble which reaches out and surrounds and envelopes everything that is as we know it, therefore is able to encompass and view everything at any moment, which means from that point of view everything is now. We are somewhere in this bubble at any moment, and whether you think today is today or not, is irrelevant...

Time only affects the material world, and as such is only measurable from something that has a beginning and an end, which is everything physical. So, time can't possibly be fixed, it varies because it's always viewed from some different viewpoint, in this case from a human perspective.

So, getting back to being in the centre of things, you would find, in a sense, that time ceases to exist, and as a result there would be no need to travel to anything, because everything would be within your bubble all at the one moment. Within this bubble of existence, both the past and the future would exist now, because in a sense as I said, there is no future or past.

It's a lot like reading a book — the beginning of the story is on page 1, and the end is on, let's say, page 350. We as a human race, are just somewhere along one of the 350 pages of the great book of life, but the whole book is already there.

By the way, this great book of life never ends!

Chapter 8

This conjures up the theory that while I am writing this book, I believe it to be 2021 but is it 2021 or is it any year or every year? We are reading this book believing that this date is the current truthful date, but in reality, it may or may not be — it's just the date we are up to at the moment, or the page in the great book of life that we are reading now.

The first thing that comes to mind here, is that if the book has been written already, then the outcome must have already been decided also.

When we are born, we have a basic blueprint of what we can and can't do. For example, we can't turn ourselves into a dog, we can't fly, we also instinctively talk through our mouths and walk on our legs. These are just examples of what I call the basic blueprint; these things can't be changed, but we do have our own free will. For example — we can make these legs we walk on go in a certain direction! Although we don't have **full** freedom, we do have enough freedom to make certain changes within our own personal lives, therefore affecting other outcomes and other people's lives/circumstances.

So yes, we can say that we are on page 25 of the great book of life for example, but we still have opportunities and free will to make our individual outcomes. This means that whilst the great book of life is written, we still can fill in the gaps.

This also could mean that there are untold numbers and variations of our future, and yet, at the same simultaneous time, before our birth or arrival on this planet… we can and do, enter any date at our choosing.

If everything is already, then all we are doing is entering some part of the great book of life and experiencing our personal choices which are being made by us.

Therefore, for everyone, our life's choices make up the personal experiences that we traverse through, in what we call our lifetime whilst here.

So, while the great book of life is already written, we still have all these choices that we can make, but as I've said, the basic blueprint is always there.

Another scenario is that whilst we think we have all these choices we may not, and we may find that we are completely programmed with the illusion of thinking that we are making our choices!

Either way, I believe we are here to have a physical experience with the emphasis on understanding emotions.

Chapter 9

When we are in the spirit world, we decide to have an experience on earth, then we choose what page of the great book of life to enter, or in other words what year we choose to experience.

When we arrive/born, we assume that the year we have arrived in, is the year that earth has evolved to, using so called time as a measurement. But that may not be correct, as the whole book of life has already been written.

The great energy force or spirit which we are all part of, exists all the time, which means everything that is passed, or in the future, is only in our imagination. The past is only a memory, and the future is only a prediction.

We believe we are singularities and that we actually are born and then die. None of these three things are correct. First of all, we are not singularities, we are part of the whole, the spirit world. In the spirit world, everything just is with no future and no past. It just is — all the time! Therefore, we exist all the time as part of the whole.

This means that our life here is simply a temporary

place, like stepping onto the stage in a big play, and then when our part is over, we step off the stage again. It is incorrect to say we are born and die, all we are really doing is transitioning to earth for an experience.

This also proves that life here is only temporary, which means this whole existence is set up purely for us to experience certain things and certain scenarios.

To imagine that life here is a major part of our existence, and to use the terminology of birth and death… is simply naïve and far too final. When the body dies, it's only our vehicle dying, we as a spiritual being are the driving force, and when the spirit leaves the body, the body can no longer operate and collapses. This can occur at any time, it all depends on what our 'mission' was. Therefore, we should never be sad that someone has left the play because it simply means their part is over, and it's time for them to go home.

Most people think that time is just a measurement of our life and is then divided up into small pieces — years, months, days, hours, minutes and seconds.

Now that is correct, but it is merely a matter of divisions, which we call by different names. This doesn't really explain what time is because we are taught that that's the way it is and so, we live our life following these terms and conditions.

For most people, it is just a simple progression from a beginning to an end, birth to death; if you like — arrival and departure I prefer to call it.

Remember, time only applies to something that has a beginning and an end.

In our material world everything has a beginning and

an end, from a blade of grass to a distant far-off star. From our point of view everything is moving and therefore has some type of deterioration; as a result, everything has a beginning and an end, but that only applies to a material world.

Chapter 10

In the old days, our early scientists used to say that a day consisted of a period from when the sun rose, to when the sun set. Obviously, it's the same today, because to change any understanding of time would create havoc, so it's easier for our governments to just let things be as they are, even if they are incorrect.

A good example of governments leaving things as they are, even if incorrect, is as follows. We are taught many things at school, i.e., maps are a typical example of how the public in general throughout the world, are being misled.

The shape of virtually every country is misrepresented on any flat map that we can lay out on a table, and they are also not represented correctly on a globe.

The real shape of most of these countries are recognisable, but quite a bit different to what is represented on a flat map — there's a reason for this inaccuracy.

Transferring the shape of a continent from a globe to a flat surface is quite difficult, so the actual shape of landmasses becomes inaccurate, but since most children are taught in schools from a flat map, the view of the shape of countries and continents has been accepted as correct, but it is not.

So, what we are taught is false, and yet we all obey the standard of our teachings.

Time is very similar in a way, because we have been taught that from our perspective everything is either older or younger, faster or slower, bigger or smaller, etc.

We have this conception because as humans we think we are all important, therefore everything must be seen from our perspective — as it was perceived in the old days, when it was thought that planet earth was the centre of the universe, and everything else revolved around it.

This as we now know, is extremely arrogant and completely wrong.

People in general do not think out-of-their-box; as a result, they stay in their box! So, things never really change, even though there is evidence to prove that things are not as they seem; time is one of those things.

Imagine for a moment that we were living on another planet where the speed of the orbit of the other planet, which we will call earth 2, was spinning at a different rate to ours, and their sun was rising and setting every six of our hours, instead of every twelve hours.

The people on earth 2, would then be dividing their day on their planet into twelve of their divisions, which they would also be calling hours.

The people there would have no concept that the hours on earth 2, were any different to the hours on our earth.

You can see where I'm going here — the time it takes for an hour to pass on earth 2, is very different to the passing of time on our earth, yet if you were born on earth 2, you would think that it was the correct and normal time. So back on our earth — we also think our time is correct; because we divide our sunrise and sunset up into twelve divisions as they do on earth 2. In either instance, both these measurements are correct for their day-to-day life!

It's now quite clear to see, that time is manufactured to suit our daily lives, and is not fixed at all. So, if time is not fixed and is variable, then it becomes impossible to determine exactly how long it may take to travel from point A to point B.

We gauge our time by how fast or slow things are going on around us, but we don't know that either. In other words, we don't really have any idea of what time is — is it going slower or faster? It all depends on what we are comparing it with.

It's simply just an inaccurate understanding, because we are constantly pitting our measurements against something that is either bigger, smaller, slower or faster; there is no way of getting any accuracy, in other words.

Our understanding of time is a bit of a farce, in fact we simply have no idea what this thing we call time really is. Time is always relative to whoever is measuring it at any moment.

In the big picture, for example in the spirit world where time moves at a totally different rate, or maybe not even at all, we would be able to compare all time periods at the same time, which again means from that view point, everything is now.

We might find that this period of existence — our lives here on this planet, although appearing to be seventy or eighty of our years, could be perhaps just a micro second in the **big** picture.

There are other ways of proving that time moves about throughout the universe. For example, when you go to sleep and have a dream, the dream often seems very long and quite drawn out; a lot of things seem to happen, but doctors have proven that while your dream seems to take a long time, the fact is, it only takes a few minutes or even less in our physical world.

The reason is, when we go to sleep, we enter a different dimension, and are therefore in a different time zone.

Even here on earth, time can be observed to sometimes move around — different people under different circumstances have had this experience. It doesn't just seem slower or faster, sometimes it actually is!

Ask any child, waiting for Christmas to come around, it seems an eternity for them, and yet ask an old person and they'll tell you that Christmas just seems like yesterday.

You could argue that that's just how different people see things but isn't that just the point!

Chapter 11

Years ago, I had a bad car accident; it was a head-on collision — and without going into the details too much, I can remember after the impact seeing the steering wheel coming up towards my head… amazingly quite slowly! I even thought I had time to get out of the way, but that didn't happen — the steering wheel kept coming, very slowly it seemed. Although I was trying to move out of the way, I wasn't quick enough, as my body was still in that same time zone as the now crumbling car. My soul or spirit had moved into a different time zone; I was now able to observe everything that was going on, albeit at a slow rate in this case.

On another separate occasion, I was doing some work around the house where I needed to use a ladder. While climbing the ladder, I lost my balance and fell off. I was only about two metres from the ground, but everything seemed to change. I can remember distinctly thinking to myself, 'when am I going to hit the ground?'.

In normal terms, the accident happened very quickly

and at a normal speed, but I was able to somehow see it from a different time zone.

So, in the big picture, how long is a second or how long is an hour?

In the spirit world, it might be equal to a hundred million years on this planet, we just don't know.

I believe that when we pass on or leave the other players on the stage of life behind — it's only then we start to realise that this life we thought was 70 or 80 years, is in fact just a drop in the bucket of spiritual or real time.

Take a piece of string for example, if all pieces of string were the same length, there would be no shorter lengths or longer lengths, they would just be simply a piece of string, because you can't have a short piece or the understanding of a short piece, unless you have a longer piece to compare it with.

It's the same concept with time, we understand that time is ticking away at a certain rate; the way we work out that rate is by comparing it to something, usually ourselves or some other fixed body, i.e., our sun for example. We are then able to work out some type of length between the two items, then we divide it up into little pieces. This doesn't mean that that's how it is everywhere. In my opinion, it is very different in almost every dimension.

So, our understanding of time and speed is just that, our understanding is a gross misconception of reality.

There are many other examples right here in front of us to prove that time is variable. Try watching a butterfly — they seem to be here about three of our days, but in those few days I think that their life is completely full; it is clear that although being on this planet, it is in a different time zone to us.

Take a house fly for example — we think that they

move around very fast, but to the house fly 'he' sees us as moving very slowly, hence when we try to swat the fly — without any effort at all, the fly has plenty of time to move away, as our hand is heading towards him very slowly from his perspective.

A tortoise crossing the road has no concept of a car passing by him at one hundred kilometres an hour, he simply does not see the car, as it is far too fast for him, so for all intents and purposes the car doesn't even exist to him, unless he is unfortunate enough to have been squashed!

Okay, so one of the difficulties we have is to understand that time as we know it isn't the same everywhere, in fact it's very different from place to place.

In the spirit world, or in our greater higher state of being, {which is where we will be and are anyway after leaving the play of life} — when there, there's no time, and so if there is no time, there can't be any movement either! At least not as we know it, because movement takes time and we've just established that there is no time. So, if there is no time — there is no movement that supports the theory that everything is right now.

If everything is right now, then there is no future or past, there is just now — and now is everything.

It is very hard for us to try and understand any of this, because our way of thinking is designed with limitations. We understand only enough to make us think that this world is totally real... Not having any memories when we arrive, we assume incorrectly that this is it!

We consider this is how everything is run in the universe, but if we understood that there was no time and everything just is, then we would probably slit our wrists and end the play, because no one would want to come to the play and act out some of the difficult parts.

We have to be restricted in our understanding, otherwise none of this thing we call life would work, because if we knew the outcome of everything, then there would be no point to any of this!

In a sense, today is the most important thing, because tomorrow from our view point hasn't happened, and the past is only a memory. This means that everything that has happened before this moment is merely a memory, and everything that is about to happen after this moment is only a possibility — so the only thing that is real for us is right now... Just a reminder, time is only a measurement of something that has a beginning and an end; if something takes what we call a long time — what exactly is a long time?

It is only long if it's compared with something that is a short time; we are calculating our time here from our viewpoint, and our viewpoint is mostly calculated on our lifespan and life style.

We make ourselves the focal point to such a degree, it makes everything seem either shorter or longer, older or younger, bigger or smaller, etc.... It all stems from our viewpoint.

Getting back to the fly, the fly sees us as massive, but we know that he is comparing us with himself, so everything we compare ourselves with, becomes either larger or smaller. As I've already said, from our viewpoint it's all relative... There is no large or small anything really, or slow or fast, it's all just our perception. So, in the great book of life, our seventy odd years here, may be barely a micro second compared to ???? in the big picture.

Chapter 12

I think that when we leave our part in the play of life, we suddenly realise that what we thought was a long time on this planet, was merely a second!

This being the case, other civilisations on other worlds may — and most probably are, on different time zones due to all sorts of reasons, such as their lifespan or their size, for example. If that is so then what may seem a long time for us, may be a short time for them.

For example, if an alien was to take a trip to our planet, it might take him let's say, a few days. In that same time period, many years may have passed here in our time.

This could explain why the distances between our planets seem so great for us, and yet for other beings it may be just a short trip.

Just imagine being an ant and having to travel to another ant nest four kilometres away — in the end, the ant may never get there in its entire lifetime; and yet for us the same four kilometres at one hundred and twenty kilometres an hour, takes us only a couple of minutes in a car. So, you can now see that time is not fixed at all, and in fact is very different everywhere.

The other thing is that time, even in our life, varies from moment to moment — one only has to look at the clock and think, 'my goodness where has the day gone.' But if you were trapped and had your leg pinned under a rock, time would seem to go much slower.

My point here is that time is relevant to different planets, dimensions and different circumstances. As shown in the previous pages here, time does in fact move around and is variable.

Take the example of when I fell off the ladder, and the time I was in the car accident when the steering wheel came up slowly towards my head, these are moments when time moves around. So, if that's the case, when a prisoner is counting out his days to his release, time is running for him at a different speed to his friend, who's just having a holiday on a beautiful island.

One could argue at this point, that a clock ticking away proves that time doesn't move, but that is incorrect. Einstein already proved that if we were travelling at the speed of light, time on earth would pass at a different speed to time in our spacecraft. That being the case, the clock in the spacecraft and the clock on earth, although manufactured in the same factory, and tick toking away at the same rate, would be recording time passing at a very different speed.

So, which clock would be correct? Either, or neither, or both. Would they just be reflecting the circumstances that they are in, proving beyond any doubt that time is not fixed and is variable?

If I was viewing all this from the spirit world, or my

higher self, I would have a much broader understanding, and I wouldn't see it as extraordinary but simply as an experience. Always remember, that we are extremely fortunate to have this opportunity to experience whatever comes our way. It should be looked upon as an adventure, not a dramatic hindrance, even though for some the part that they play can be very physically hard.

Chapter 13

So, what does this all mean to us? Just having some understanding of what is going on, helps us enormously because we then start to realise that this experience is just that, an experience. When we understand that, we then start to place less emphasis on our material gains, and more emphasis on our spiritual awareness.

As we all know, at the end of the day nothing material can be taken with us anyhow. I find it bewildering when I see people placing so much emphasis on their material gains.

Knowing a little of what is going on, gives us direction, so we can try to understand just what and why, in this so-called reality, is occurring.

Our part in the play, or life as we call it that we have been given, is nothing short of extraordinary. That is from my understanding, but I am only a material mortal, at the moment.

If I was viewing this from my spiritual self, or my higher self, then I would have a much broader understanding. I wouldn't see it as extraordinary, but simply as an experience.

If everybody was taught this at home, and also in early school, how important it is to advance spiritually, the world would be a very different place.

If we placed as much emphasis on our spiritual advancement as we do on our material gains, we would have greater understanding of each other — with little or no competitiveness. This would culminate in peace and harmony, coupled with no greed; hence there would be no wars. An amazing turnaround for the human race would occur.

Always remember that we are extremely fortunate to have this opportunity to experience whatever comes our way; it should be looked upon as an adventure, not a dramatic hindrance, even though for some, the part that they play can be very physically arduous. So having some understanding of what's going on helps us enormously, because we then start to realise that this experience is just that, an experience. When we understand that, we start to place less emphasis on our material gains, and more emphasis on our spiritual awareness.

Chapter 14

When I was a little boy, I often felt that even though I seemed to be alone, I was never really alone. I was aware that there was someone or something always around me, watching me, observing my every action. The thing is, while I thought this was normal, I never discussed this with any of my friends, as I feared they might think I was stupid.

Of course, I know now, my awareness of someone being around me was not in my imagination, but was in fact my higher self, or what sometimes people call their spiritual guides. It doesn't matter what you call them, but what is important is to be aware that you are never alone. There is always help for you no matter what situation you might find yourself in.

Placing less emphasis on material values and more on spiritual values, you will find that material loss in your life — which sometimes occurs, doesn't have the devastating impact it may have had before. So, these material crises in our life tend to be easier to handle due to your new understanding; that these events are only there for our experience.

Material things are nice to have, and quite important as this is a material world/play.

But understand their true values, they must never be allowed to override our value of our spiritual advancement, and the spiritual values that come with it. After all, at the end of the day/play, wisdom is the only thing we take with us. Hence, any wisdom gained from our material experiences are the most important reasons we are here for.

On thinking further about this, one wonders what this world is really like… For example, I have a classic car, and most people think that it's beautiful — but if a bull walked into my shed, all he would see is an obstacle in his way — and without any doubt would probably kick the car not realising it was special to me.

What we see isn't always as it is — we may see a flower as a brilliant yellow and red, while a bee sees the same flower as a brilliant black and silver, so who is correct? The bee or the human? If we were able to ask an ant and an elephant what they saw when looking at the same picture in front of them, we would get a very different answer — both see very different things for lots of reasons. One of the reasons is because they are programmed differently, the other reason is their size; it would all be determined differently from each creature's perception.

So, what is it that we are really looking at, and who is correct — the bee, the elephant, or the human? In a sense, we don't really know what is real and what is not real, because we all see the same thing with different values, hence different priorities. So, the world isn't as we humans see it necessarily. We expect all the creatures to understand the way we see things, because we feel we are superior, but of course this is incorrect, we are not superior.

It seems to me, the picture we see is quite different to what other creatures see — we think that a bear coming in stealing the food out of our garbage bins, must see us as superior having a nice home etc. But that's not necessarily the case, he simply sees food!

When an animal is hunting, take a tiger for instance, do you think for a moment that he sees a human and says, wait a minute that's a human, I can't eat them — they are special.

The tiger sees us as nothing more or less than he is programmed to — food, so makes no special avoidances whether we are human or animal! It makes no difference to the tiger when he's so hungry!

So, if this planet isn't as it seems, and it is different for every species depending on their viewpoint, then it is highly likely that all of what we think we know about our universe / space, is also not necessarily as we see it, and highly likely to be very different for everything and everyone. That being the case, we actually have no idea what is out there or here, because we only see what we're programmed to see; as a result, we only believe what we're programmed to believe. It would be extremely arrogant and naive to suggest we have a handle on things, because I believe we have no idea of what is going on and what isn't!

Chapter 15

Some nights ago, I watched an old Star Trek Voyager movie. In the movie, the Voyager spaceship was caught somehow in the orbit of a planet while they did some repairs. Whilst the repairs were taking place, they discovered that there was a society on the planet they were orbiting, albeit at a very early stage in development. Anyhow, in the movie, they soon realised that there was an enormous time difference between themselves and the planet below.

After careful analyses, they discovered that the planet and the civilisation were progressing at three months per second of the Voyager's time.

While the Voyager was orbiting for a couple of days doing repairs, in that time several thousand years had passed on the planet! A whole civilisation on this planet had gone from prehistoric, to a more advanced space capability than Voyager currently had.

Obviously, all sorts of things happened due to this fact.

My point here is that we think we understand time and

that time is fixed, and in our arrogance, we think time is moving at a certain rate and therefore everything else must be either slower or faster — this is totally incorrect, this is the way humans think. So, it conjures up the idea, that if on some planets time is running at a very different rate to others, that the theory would also be the same in different dimensions; in other words, a physical dimension or a spiritual dimension — that type of thing. Like the bees and the humans, we both see the colour of flowers differently. It's the same with our observation of time, which speed is the correct speed — the faster one, or the slower one, or the current speed?

There is no truth in saying any one of these is correct, because they are all correct for their situation. But I believe they're all just aspects attached to the different plays, which are playing out in different dimensions and worlds.

This is particularly hard to understand, or to even try and explain it — because it is so out of the box thinking, but I am sure that this is what's going on. Hence time is merely a tool that is used to divide up our life into little bits…

From where we stand, life can appear to be quite a long time, but since we have nothing to compare it with, the whole of humanity and the earth, viewed from a central spiritual point — where time doesn't exist — maybe all established and finished in a nanosecond!

Chapter 16

I know I have spoken about this before, but I will reiterate here that our spiritual world and our physical world are linked. They work together, simultaneously reflecting each other in a sense, a bit like a hand in a glove — the glove represents the body, and the hand represents the spirit; one needs the other to operate correctly. Remove the hand from the glove and the glove becomes useless, never to move again until the hand / spirit returns.

Try to imagine, there is a godlike figure, or creator, or a central spiritual point — {whatever you want to call it,} in the centre of everything, and everything else is revolving around it. In the centre of this enormous bubble, it encompasses everything, which includes all universes, and all spaces everywhere, and everything as we know it — the whole of space with all universes and all solar systems and planets revolving around each other! From that point of view, the 'creator' in the centre can view everything at the one time, therefore is able to touch or be involved with everything at the one time. For 'it', everything just is — as all is revolving around a focal point, hence there would be no time. However, for each universe that's moving around, there is time, because it takes time to move!

Everything is revolving around something else in this enormous bubble, right down to the tiniest thing we know about, such as an atom, which is a millionth the size of a grain of sand. Now there are even smaller things that orbit the atom. Where does it begin and where does it end? Well, it doesn't, there is no time from certain viewpoints, e.g., the creator's viewpoint, but where anything has movement, there is time.

Secondly, time is very different in different worlds due to all sorts of reasons, but particularly those of size and speed, and their movements of spin/rotation etc.

Chapter 17

We all experience dreams every night, but on most occasions, we don't even remember them the next day until maybe something triggers our memory, and we suddenly say, that's just broken a dream I had last night. The question is what exactly are dreams and how important are they to us?

Our 'normal' days are broken into three periods: one is a sleeping period of approximately eight hours; the other is our working period, again, of approximately eight hours; and thirdly, is a period in which we hopefully spend time for ourselves.

In this physical realm in which we exist, our priority is to live, which includes feeding ourselves so that the physical being can go on. We usually end up at the end of our working day fairly tired, as a result don't have a lot of time for ourselves, and when we do have some time, we are usually too tired, and go off to bed. We awake the next morning hopefully refreshed, and on we go off to do the same thing again and again.

Now if this is so important, and it takes up most of our awake hours, why do we have to spend roughly eight hours every day asleep? Why is it so important that our Creator has made it so?

I've heard the usual explanation that the body has to rest for eight hours in order to recover, so it can go back to work again the next day. While this may be true for the physical body, where does our spirit go during our sleep period and what does it do?

Our dreams seem to be divided into categories...

1... some dreams appear to be worry dreams, dreams that are connected to our concerns of the day.

2... some dreams may be sexual in content which again relates back to our concerns of the day.

3... some dreams, if you're fortunate, can be messages sent in the form of premonitions.

4... some dreams just seem totally confusing and don't really make much sense.

5... some dreams can be a follow-through of our personal wishes.

6... There are many, many other categories that dreams could fall into — take for example, dreams that seem to be in another place or time. When you were there it seemed so real, so real in fact, that when you awaken from the dream, you can be disappointed — finding that you are still here on planet Earth.

We know how important it is to work for our living, we also know how important it is to have personal time out and recreation, but most people don't realise how important it is for us to have dream periods, we just seem to take it for granted. As the body needs food and rest to recover from work, so the spirit also needs to be reconnected to its home, in order to replenish its energy source and continue working together in harmony. Hence both do this at the same time — we call it sleep, and it's absolutely essential to both the spirit and the body of all creatures, as every creature has a soul that's part of the spirit world.

Chapter 18

The concept of other dimensions...

There are a few possibilities, for instance where do UFOs come from? Are they all from outer space, or are they us from the future? Are there 'black ops' being hidden from the public? Are UFOs from planet Earth, or from a different dimension?

I suppose I should say here that all of these scenarios are possible, for example aliens travelling to earth to visit us. It's one of the most common thoughts that UFOs come from other planets, and it's highly likely of course — but most people think that if they came from other planets they would have to travel for a very long time.

It's no doubt obvious that this is incorrect — it's all to do with time and distance again. If the aliens are on a different time frame to us for example, one of their weeks could be equal to let's say, ten of our years here on earth — then their spacecraft would only have to travel a few of their weeks, in order to come such great distances without it taking a long time. It's my guess that time is not the same everywhere across the universe, this would account for the ability of other spacecraft to travel what are considered enormous distances without spending years to do it. I am also of the opinion that these great distances are not necessarily as great as we assume they are.

Let's go back to around the 1600s when competition was rife between European countries for the East Indies trade. Spain, England and Portugal were all in great competition for the spices from Southeast Asia.

Sailing from Europe to Southeast Asia was a long trip, and the navigation in those days was misunderstood. The main problem was that when sea charts were first made of our Earth, the chart makers had to reproduce a plan on a flat map!

Now, because we know the world is round, producing an accurate map direction-wise, onto a flat surface, and relating it to a sphere, left much room for inaccuracies.

Almost all sea charts today are produced on flat maps, and most charts only cover fairly small areas, which means the curvature doesn't take this into consideration; there is still a continuing job of correcting your course, due to numerous other things, but in particular trying to follow a curved line with a straight line which is not possible. These early charts, and the charts of today, are still called Mercator charts. It wasn't until the Portuguese realised, and then designed a chart that took into account curved lines — these were called gnomonic charts. When the Portuguese started making charts with curved lines instead of straight, they realised that they were able to get from Europe to the Far East, clipping a couple of weeks off the trip!

This meant that when a ship was sailing towards a point on a map, it went straight for a certain distance, and then made a correction and went straight again.

This was very inaccurate because many straight lines were loaded with many corrections. This meant it wasn't the quickest or the shortest route, as it didn't take into account the curvature of the world because the sailors then were using flat maps/charts.

When the Portuguese discovered and worked out how to go from A to B following a curved line, it enabled the Portuguese to get from Europe to Southeast Asia ahead of the ships' arrivals from Spain and the UK. As a result, this discovery was top secret for a long time.

A great circle is the longest line that can be drawn around the earth. A segment of a great circle is the shortest distance between two points on the earth's surface. When planning ocean passages, small scale 'gnomonic' charts can be used to calculate great circle routes. On longer passages, ships can save fuel by sailing the shorter great circle route. On a Mercator projection chart, lines of latitude are parallel, as are lines of longitude.

A rhumb line course of 040° crosses each meridian, (lines of longitude) at the same angle. A rhumb line course is used in all coastal navigation. If a passage is over six hundred miles, it may be quicker to sail a great circle route.

My point here, is that everything in space being round — the chances are that there will be shortcuts from A to B, rather than following the long route which is exactly what happened in the 1600s. So, in saying this, it is my guess that aliens not only are living in a different time frame, but also have the knowledge of the shortcuts through space.

This is just normal navigation — I'm not talking here about star gates, and wormholes, and black holes etc., they are very different again.

Chapter 19

The possibility that the spacecrafts, or at least some of them, are not necessarily all alien — they could be humans coming back from what we understand to be the future. Now, if we assume as I said before, we are currently in the year 2021, and that is correct, but it may not be the current year — what is the current year if all years have come and gone? Just like a book of ten thousand pages, for example we are on page 2021, but as we can see, there are many pages in front of us. These pages are what we call future, and the pages before 2021 become the past, for us at least.

I believe that when we are in the spirit world, we can enter this book of life at any period, because from the spirit world — all is at once. So, for us to come into the great book of life as I call it, to experience something, we have the choice of coming to any period or any time. That being the case, when we arrive here or born as we call it, we assume that this is where civilisation is up to, and that is correct for us at that moment.

In my opinion, I think that when you're a spirit and you

decide to have an experience somewhere in this great book of life, the particular circumstances and situations that are necessary could be at any time in any family.

It may be that you enter the great book of life anywhere along the timeline, to experience a situation and/or certain circumstances that you wish — or need to do.

So, we have no way of knowing whether the year that we are in is the current year! What is the current year if everything just 'IS' NOW? The idea of there being no future or past, and everything being all at once, is very hard to get your head around — until you look at everything from a viewpoint of outside. In other words, if you look at a complete book you see all the pages at once, and this explains the unnecessary need for time.

Time is only something that we use to dissect something else that has a beginning and an end. But if everything is — there is no beginning and no end because it's all cyclical. Imagine for a moment that bubble again, imagine it floating out of a bath tub. Look at the bubble carefully, and ask yourself 'where does it begin, and where does it end?'.

It seems to me that there is a very high possibility that some of the spacecraft that we see from time to time, are in fact humans from what we call the future. Naturally, we would expect on page 5000 of the great book of life, that humans have developed the ability to traverse through what we commonly call time.

Chapter 20

As we know, the human race in its development has been lied to, and tricked and misled by many, i.e., governments, financial institutions, multinationals, and religions of all sorts. For various reasons, and mostly to control the masses to keep them busy, therefore unable to have the time to even think, let alone challenge the small minority who are controlling the masses.

To control the populations easily, fear is the greatest tool — both governments and religions use fear to control the masses. Think about it for a moment, if you break man's law, the government will have the right to put you in jail. Religion uses the same trick also... If you do the wrong thing, you'll go to hell. Fear is taught first thing when you're a child — you get told things like, 'if you're naughty you'll go to bed without your dinner, or you'll get a smack on your bottom', etc. It's the carrot and stick effect, and it has been used, and will be used on us, until we do something to change it.

We are also controlled with our workload, for example

— the workload is often so great, in order just to feed and house ourselves, we find we have to work most of our waking hours. This means of course, that when we're finished working, we hardly have any time for ourselves. When you think about it, we sleep seven to eight hours out of the twenty-four. We work at least eight hours, and usually more, for somebody else, and then another couple of hours is taken up travelling to and from our jobs! When that's over, there are a few hours spent during the day filling your stomach. Then, if you're 'lucky', you may have an hour or two to chat with your family.

This control is designed to keep us busy to such a degree, that we don't seem to have any time for the most important thing on the planet, which is our spiritual development.

Chapter 21

The development of electronics and artificial intelligence is already a long way ahead of what the public are allowed knowledge of and are able to buy. For example, if you buy a new mobile phone, you assume that it's the latest technology, but it's not. The technology is at least five years ahead of what the public are being fed to know about, and the technology devices that are used, or will be used in wars to come, are very much top secret, and a long way ahead of what the public knows or realises.

As a result, some of these strange looking aircraft that look like a UFO, are in fact test flights, with flying machines far superior to what we are currently used to seeing in our skies normally... hence we think it's a UFO.

A UFO from a different dimension on earth.

Consider for a moment that there are numerous other dimensions here on planet Earth that exist simultaneously. This, in my opinion, is very likely.

How many times have we heard of people suddenly seeing things and then later found they're not there? This has happened quite a lot throughout the ages; you can read about it in numerous stories from different people around the world.

What's happened here? How can people see something that isn't there? People see ghosts and assume that they are dead people; this may be right, but it could also be a flash vision from something from another dimension here on earth.

If you think this is a little far-fetched — if you can't see it, it's not there, think again...

Can you see the air? The answer is no, but it is definitely present.

Can you see electricity? No, but it is definitely felt.

Can we see thought? No, but it is definitely there.

When you think about it, there are more things in the unknown world that we don't know about than we know, and these are all things we can't see. If the majority of things that exist are invisible to us, why would it be so far-fetched to think that there are numerous different dimensions? I can think of one that everybody knows something about, that is the spirit world. The spirit world is quite clearly in a different dimension, we cannot see it but almost all of us realise it exists.

There are numerous spots throughout the world, commonly known as grids. One of the most well-known is the Bermuda Triangle. In the Bermuda Triangle there have been recordings of many strange happenings, so much so, that there have been numerous books written about this phenomenon, and quite a few movies. One of the most famous stories was when a flight of World War 11 airplanes, disappeared without the slightest trace — where did they go?

This is a question that has been asked numerous times, and many people have come up with different theories. I think these areas, known as grids, where strange phenomena happen, are in fact spots where it's possible via natural phenomena, to pass into another dimension. These dimensions I believe, are of a slightly different frequency/dimension, and the vibration of everything is also different to ours. As a result, this allows different dimensions to exist in the same space yet being unable to be aware or conscious of each other's dimensions. This idea allows for numerous civilisations to be existing side-by-side in the same space/time, and yet separately.

I believe that some of these sightings, UFOs in particular, are actually glimpses of flying aircraft from a different dimension but living side-by-side with us. As a rule, we probably should not be able to see them, then one would assume that they probably don't see us most of the time. However occasionally, the governing rules of being separate, breakdown allowing both sides to get a glimpse of each other, albeit not really clearly, but nevertheless a glimpse of each other.

Chapter 22

Imagine there are ten artists from ten different dimensions, commissioned to paint on a massive piece of glass, a scene representing their world — as they know it. Each artist has painted a beautiful scene on glass of their world. We are now able to look at the painting and its beauty, and for all intents and purposes it is solid. However, we don't realise it's on glass, until we see a little area where the artist hasn't put quite enough paint on! Upon closer examination, we are able to get a glimpse through the glass — where we see another painting on the glass, very different to ours.

The artist's work on the second sheet of glass, he and his brush, are vibrating at a slightly different speed to us; as a result, the picture that we see is not as clear as what we're used to. The second sheet of glass/painting of the other world, also has 'weaknesses' here and there, and if one was able to look through the weaknesses — you would see yet another painting of another world, and so on and so on.

This is just a childlike example of how several different worlds can be living in the same space-time area. This being the case, this planet is a very different place to our current understanding. I believe we have numerous dimensions living side-by-side here unknowingly to each other.

Over the years, there has been a lot of discussion about aliens visiting this planet; it seems almost always we assume that the aliens have come from another planet, but what if they haven't? What if they are here living on this planet but in a slightly different dimension?

Now, I've mentioned this before, but I'll try and explain it a little better.

Take a flat surface for example, say a page on a picture book — when you look at the page it may appear to have depth, but when you look at the page's edge, it's then you realise that it has no depth.

This is a two-dimensional field; if you were a character on that page you would only be able to see back or forth, or sideways. In your two-dimensional world you would not be able to comprehend another dimension such as up, for example.

If someone asked you to look up you wouldn't understand what is up, because up is another dimension that you have no idea about.

In your two-dimensional world that you live in, if someone came along and tried to appear to you from a third dimension — i.e., up, you wouldn't be able to see them until they arrived on your flat piece of paper, your world.

When and if they did appear, you would only see them as a two dimensional 'thing', in other words you would see them as a flat line!

Therefore, you would not be able to see their real shape or appearance, because they would come from a different dimensional world.

Living in your two-dimensional world, you would find it almost impossible to understand or to recognise a third dimension. You would never see it for what it is, therefore, you would misinterpret the visitor shape and size altogether, seeing it only as a line. You may not even notice it at all.

We live in a three-dimensional world so we have the third dimension and are able to see it quite easily because our brains are set up for that, but if there was a fourth, fifth or sixth dimension we would be unable to comprehend and certainly unable to see it.

From where we stand, we would assume it doesn't exist unless we are open-minded to other possibilities.

It's quite possible in my opinion, that other beings are occupying the same space that we are living in, but they are likely to be in another dimension, which means we would never be able to see them, but they would almost certainly be able to see us.

I think that there are numerous civilisations living simultaneously in this same space that we occupy.

Let's assume for a moment there are seven or eight dimensions occupying the same space — the civilisation on the eighth dimension say, would be able to see all, but the civilisation on the seventh dimension — would only be able to see themselves — and of course the lower numbers.

As for us, we can only see and be in these three dimensions — but of course we have a thorough understanding of two dimensions — i.e., flat!

That being said, you would think that the beings on the eighth or seventh dimension would be very concerned about the insane things that are happening in the third dimension:

— ours, such as wars using nuclear bombs, etc.

They wouldn't want us doing crazy things with atomic warfare because it would almost certainly have an effect on their civilisation, and all the civilisations in between.

We call ourselves civilised, and yet we can't see anything which lies out of our understanding; we just assume if we can't see it, then it mustn't exist.

Just for a moment, imagine holding a live electricity wire — nothing happens, but it is definitely there.

Explaining some of the UFO sightings — {often not very clear, because they're on a different vibration speed.} Their world to them appears normal, and our world would appear blurry.

It also explains the strange happenings in the grids, the Bermuda Triangle for example, it also explains people seeing ghosts, again — are they ghosts or are they people from another dimension living side-by-side with us?

If this is correct and there are numerous civilisations here in the same space-time, then we have a much greater responsibility for looking after our planet, and not messing around with powerful weapons, that may destroy not only our human race, but all the creatures living in this dimension and possibly numerous other dimensions.

Chapter 23

Is it possible that the spirit leaves the body each night when we go to what we call sleep? The spirit goes to the spirit world, and then the following day, or even just after a catnap, the spirit returns. If the spirit isn't a single phenomenon, and is all one within the spirit world, the spirit that returns after you've had a sleep, may not be exactly the same individual spirit as before. It's a bit like a taxi — the taxi has a different driver every day, but for the mechanic who looks after the taxi, he sees only the taxi with the same problems all the time, even though the driver is different each day.

So, when we look at a person, its physical body looks and responds the same as it did yesterday, i.e., acts the same, has the same memories and idiosyncrasies, etc. How would anybody know if there was a change of drivers? We all just assume because the body looks the same, it must be the same or have the same driver.

This could explain why we see changes in people from day to day — the spirit may be different, as the result then could reflect our view of the body.

In this life we all assume everything is as we view it, or as our five senses inform us, but that's not necessarily what is happening.

I'm sure we have all noticed over our history that before an invention is made or discovered, we often hear about it in science fiction stories, films or books, or even made-up stories. I can think of numerous stories — take 20,000 Leagues Under the Sea, written in the 19th century. He wrote about submarines sixty or seventy years before they were starting to build these submarines.

So, what does that mean? Do we get the thought first before we do anything? Answer — always. That means that the inventions we make, always follow the thought that was received some time before. Now if that's the case, then we are inventing things and going a certain direction because we have received a thought. We then unintentionally follow the idea, we call it when it becomes a physical reality a 'discovery'. Hence one can assume from this that the thought is being sent, then we convert it into what we call our reality.

That's one way of looking at it; what if we are in effect creating our own reality from our own thoughts? For example, a person thinks of an idea and without realising it, actually manifests the idea. It's not just the idea/theory that is manifested, it can be and is anything and everything.

Is it just a coincidence that the sightings of UFOs have expanded enormously since we have had the understanding and the idea of possible space flight? It seems strange to me, that for thousands of years we have not known how to fly, or even had any realisation of flight with the odd exception

— but once we were developing flight and realised that we may be able to go to the stars, we then wondered if there are other beings out there. As soon as we started to wonder, then we started to see more UFOs, then we create the possibility of things like UFOs, assuming this is as I say, everything we assume — is not, until we create! That being the case, whatever is out there is what we are yet to create.

If I'm correct, we need to get a handle on our thoughts, because the negative things we think about are creating and making life much more difficult than necessary. This may seem like a bizarre theory, but if I am correct — let's face it, the theory certainly seems to have a lot of support, hence we are in fact godlike beings creating our future path by our own thinking.

I propose that both these scenarios are true to a degree because there is no doubt the energy that is running our bodies/organic machines, is spirit in its pure essence, therefore belonging to the over used word — God.

This means that we are very much in charge of what is, and what has been, and will be happening in what we call the future. All these ideas I have put to you are just theories, but they all make sense, therefore must all be taken seriously.

It's nice to theorise, but at the end of the day things are what they are, so it doesn't matter what religion or what you believe in, because the outcome when you pass away, is the same! In a sense, following any particular religion is really a waste of time in my opinion.

After writing about all these theories of what may or may not be, there should be certain things that are quite clear to the reader by now; one thing for sure, is that we are definitely controlled by our spirit. That being the case, the body is only a biological vehicle, so it makes this place only temporary, from our personal viewpoint — because we arrive and then we leave, as in birth and death. We should then look at the reasons why we are here — is it just random? I don't think so; it seems to me that we are here to experience many situations — a learning curve, enabling us to progress spiritually; we are here also to allow the spirit to experience this physical 3D way of existence. I believe that in the spirit world, we obviously don't have physical feelings, and also emotions to cope with as we do here.

This physical experience involves both; hence it would be quite a test to the spirit that enters, to experience the physical body and its emotions for the first time.

Chapter 24

Years ago, I carved onto an old piece of driftwood the words: 'LISTEN TO YOURSELF, FOR YOU ARE YOUR OWN GUIDE'. I gave it to my daughter who was fifteen at the time. She's now married with three children and still treasures it. That little voice you hear is yourself, or your higher self as I like to call it. Our existence here can be considered like a play — in this play we have a role, and when our part is over, we get to go home — our true home.

Any advice on which direction to take in life, is usually gleaned from our parents/guardians, and our upbringing in general. Intuition doesn't play much of a part in it usually, but it should — it should be part of the curriculum, in my opinion we should be teaching our children about the power of the spirit and mind, and about what is really going on.

All we are ever taught it seems, is about what's going on in the material world — it's almost as though there is no spiritual world; how naive is that? Our soul is the body's driver or helmsman, and without it the body would just drop to the ground, so it makes sense to learn about the driver and what it is capable of. The soul is our driver and our guide; we should be listening and acting on what it says all the time — remember that little voice?

Life is very much like a book — it has already been written. The proof is the fact that some people can see into what we call the future. All they are really doing however is skipping a few pages, to have a look ahead at the possibilities and probabilities within the following chapters... Also, in saying that, life is about choices — we make our own path as we travel along this journey. There is really no right or wrong path, there is just a multitude of choices, therefore a multitude of outcomes/consequences; whether we make them or only think we make them, it's our experience of them.

We arrive here and play our small part in this incredible book — going from page to page, chapter to chapter, year after year. As we progress, our physical bodies get older and older. We call this a passage of time or a life. Don't forget, this book of choices has already been written, and all we are doing is acting out our version of it, determined by the decisions we make whether they be logical or intuitive.

The logical way makes more immediate sense to most, and it sometimes seems easier to follow, but it is not the best way to live an interesting life, full of experiences and surprises. The intuitive way (not to be confused with being a fatalist), is more testing, because some of the time the decisions we make don't make much sense at the time — hence they are impossible to justify because we can't see the outcome like the spirit can; so, we plod along on the left brain's logical track. If we knew what was around the corner, we probably wouldn't do half of the things we do!

If you want to develop your connection with the spirit or soul, then it's only a matter of listening, **trusting** and acting. It's all about trust — if you trust in the natural intuitive system, then life becomes easier and much more interesting and enjoyable, with many good outcomes.

It says in the Bible, that man was made in God's image, and most people think that this statement means that we must look like God, or God must look like us! Therefore, they assume that God may look like an old mature man with a grey beard etc. I think what the statement means, is that we are all parts of the one source.

Take the design of a car for example, it was designed by man but looks nothing like a man, although in a way it does resemble man in that it has four wheels — a human has two legs and two arms. The car has two headlights — a human has two eyes. The car has a grill at the front, resembling a mouth if you like, and in the same position the engine is the heart. And so, the car resembles a man, yet looks nothing like him.

When we meet somebody for the first time, we sometimes get a feeling that we already know that person, and sometimes they may feel the same way. Yet we are both sure we have never met before. I believe that these two people do actually know each other, and the souls recognise each other from the spirit world, the real world.

Some people call this chemistry, and to be fair part of it is chemistry, because the two physical bodies understand there is a connection. Other people use the term soulmate, which is also correct. When we meet someone that we feel we know or have known, there is recognition of some sort that passes between the two souls, then converted to a feeling the two bodies understand. Many people call this feeling chemistry.

Imagine two people that already know each other quite well, and unbeknown to each other, they both go to the same fancy dress party. They bump into each other at the party, not realising they would both be there. At first they don't recognise each other through their physical eyes, because of their 'costumes.' But they soon realise that there is something familiar, so they ask, "don't I know you from somewhere?" or perhaps, "haven't we met before?" When two souls meet that know each other, the feeling is converted to the physical body, but at a fancy dress party — doubt leaves us unsure.

When you get to know somebody well, you tend to look past their physical appearance; you see in your mind's eye the real person, or the soul. This proves that we are spiritual beings wearing a costume… i.e., the physical body.

In Australia, sometimes when it's really hot, if I get the chance, I go to the cinema to see a movie and enjoy the air-conditioned comfort. It's often just an excuse to catch up on a movie that I had missed. But after sitting in air-conditioned comfort watching a gripping movie that maybe set in a colder climate, I'm often quite surprised when I go outside again to find it is still hot and sunny! It's a very different place.

Life here in the physical is very much like that. We arrive and act out our part in the play, and when the play is over, we leave and go back to our real world, the spirit world. The fact that we have to arrive (birth) and leave (death) — to act here in this life/play, tells me it cannot possibly be the main or real part of our existence. This play is so well constructed, we feel it is real, and in a sense, things are real in the play!

Imagine for a moment we were one of the characters in the movie, and the movie was our only and real world. The movie would have to be running all the time for us to exist indefinitely, but it isn't — it has a beginning and an end, therefore proving that this is not our real world, just a temporary place we visit to experience 'situations'.

The driver or the soul **never** dies — it is absolutely necessary to operate the body and make it move. The soul and our physical body work very closely together, intermingling in harmony. As the body needs food and rest to recover from daily activities etc., so the spirit also needs to be reconnected to its home, — source, to replenish its energy, whilst continuing working together in harmony.

We call it sleep, it's absolutely essential to both the spirit and the body amongst all creatures — as you know every creature has a soul which is part of the spirit/energy world.

We need to remind ourselves often, that while we have individual bodies here, we are ONE in the 'real' permanent world. Therefore, every time we hurt, degrade, or even kill, we are doing it to ourselves! We have to stop thinking as individuals and remember that we are all ONE in absolute reality.

The spirit world where everything is forever, is our true home. In the spirit world there is no time, as time only affects things with a beginning and an end making the spirit world a place that is always — and always is.

Imagine if you were to cut up a book and lay the pages out one after the other, there would be a beginning and an end, and also there would be a distance between the first page and the last page. So, it would take time to read the pages because you would travel a certain distance between the first and last page — which takes time. That's how this play called life is set up here.

Now imagine the spirit world where all the pages of this incredible book are not flowing one after the other but are stacked on **top** of each other. Also imagine that they are transparent so you can look into all the pages of the big story at the same time — you would be able to see it all. That's what I mean about there being no time in the spirit world, everything just IS RIGHT NOW. Try looking at it in the following scenario. Imagine a wave in the ocean, now consider that what is behind the wave or following the wave, is the past — the crest of the wave is NOW, and the rest of the wave that appears to be pushed along in front, is the future. So, my point is, the only thing that's really happening is what is happening now… The water that's following the wave is the past, therefore is only a memory that does not exist any more. The water in front of the wave being pushed along, is only a possibility and does not exist as it hasn't happened yet. The only thing that really is happening is on the crest of the wave which is right now.

We enter the great book at some stage or chapter; we act out our version as we go along. The play is written, but we make up the words and our own lines as we go. There are endless opportunities throughout this journey. The whole procedure is called life and it's amazing! Life can be very stimulating, interesting and exciting if we allow ourselves to follow our own personal guidance. If you listen, you will realise it is trying to talk to you all the time.

We call the little voice we hear in our heads by many different names. Some people call it intuition, others call it guidance from above, or our higher self, or even God. I think it is the spiritual side of ourselves we hear, that's our own spirit talking to us and advising us.

Obviously, these messages do not come in a loud verbal voice, but in the form of thoughts and feelings, and that is why many people find it difficult to determine the difference between these and the regular thoughts from the left brain. But the more you listen and respond to your personal guide, the more messages you will receive.

After a while, you learn to tell the difference between spiritual advice and logical thinking — it just comes naturally because it is the natural and the correct way. Moreover, it doesn't really matter what you like to call it, it's all the same, it's the little voice that is always with you trying to help. The reason we usually don't take notice, is because there are two sides to our brain, the left side is the logical side, and the right side is the intuitive creative side. The conflict begins when a thought comes to us — we either act on it (right brain), or we start to analyse it (left brain).

The latter immediately creates doubts, and when you have doubts it usually pollutes the thought stream; you start to begin to analyse the pros and cons, then we start to modify the thought. It isn't long before the thought has changed altogether! We now have a new thought from the left logical brain which may or may not work out, but you have just missed a possibility of using a better track… But you'll never know!

Chapter 25

There are many ways to go on our journey through life, many different roads that we can travel on, which is exactly the way it is meant to be. We are almost totally influenced and controlled by the way society is set up i.e., education, the need to seek the best job, bringing up children with the so called 'right' beliefs, having a certain type of house in the best suburb, or driving the latest car, and so on.

All these pressures are dictated to us as being the 'correct' way to go about life, they **seem** logical. So, we almost always follow the logical way, because everyone else is going that way — so it seems correct, right? Well, what really happens is we become predictable, as in a football game. If we know which way the player is going to turn and run with that precious ball he's holding, then he is easy to tackle.

Business people and governments all take advantage of this 'weakness' — yes, I say weakness because we don't trust ourselves, as a result we become very easily manipulated. The big boys throw in a little fear, which is then whipped up by the media, and in no time they have us jumping through hoops. The only way these business people and governments can control us so easily, is because we invariably take the logical way, so we become **very** predictable, therefore easy to control.

We are all in this trap to one degree or another. When I realised what was going on with my right and left brain, I decided to try my hardest to use my right brain for most of the decisions I make — it's working well!

Don't forget, governments and big businesses cannot survive without us, — the population that works for them, in fact, without us, they wouldn't even exist!

I'm not saying here that we don't need businesses, we do need them because of the way this society is set up. But I intensely dislike the control and manipulation that big business and governments wield over us.

They need us so they can survive, therefore we should and must control them. The so-called rules or laws they design are meant to keep us working, therefore under their control. They don't allow us to have hardly any time for ourselves to mature spiritually.

The system has gone full circle; the very governments that we voted in to work for us, now have us working for them! Remember, we are caretakers while we are here, we do not own anything really, but it's worth being reminded that everything we think we own, will sooner or later be taken from us — even if it's just when we leave the play! We place far too much value on our material possessions, and at the same time we place very little value on our spiritual development. Some people would practically sell their soul for material gain, while spiritually they are in reverse gear! We should constantly remind ourselves that this is only a play, and when we leave the stage, we leave everything behind. All these so-called possessions we foolishly think we own, are in fact only props for the play. We need to enjoy the ride and not be too materialistic or emotionally affected by the other actors in the play.

Due to the constant drive of big business and governments, parents today are often forced to hire people to look after their children because they are so busy. I know for sure that hired help cannot, and will not, bring a child up with the same values as a dedicated parent.

The examples our governments set are terrible, for instance the government may tell you they are trying to stop war, while at the very same time they are busy manufacturing and selling arms to the armies that are fighting. What sort of example is that? Any wonder half the population is running off the rails in confusion.

We are trained/indoctrinated from the word go. Children watch cartoons on TV that are violent to one degree or another — at the very least wield a seductive influence. On top of all that, there is religious indoctrination which does nothing but segregate the population. How childish it is for people to argue between each other about what their God may have said, e.g., my God said this, or my God said that. It's gone so far that people are prepared to kill each other over some petty argument.

It's the type of argument you would expect to hear from five-year-old school children in the school playground. Religion should be left at home. Wouldn't it be fantastic if all people took the intuitive track in life so governments, big business and religion would be unable to control and manipulate us? We would be unpredictable, and life would be so different and so much better.

Chapter 26

The window to gaining knowledge is there for everybody. Some people get the message in dreams, others get what they call premonitions, but it's all the same. The most important thing is to act on your personal message. If you don't, you will probably find yourself on the wrong track. Not acting/responding to what you hear, is the same as denying you have a spirit. You are also closing the door to any more messages. The more you respond to your personal messages, the more often the door opens for you, and the better life will be for you.

Have you ever noticed when you're around certain people, you often get a strong feeling of perhaps caution or fear, or maybe that you feel you know the person? These feelings are sensors your soul picks up to alert you via your physical body. Just imagine for a moment that the whole of the Earth is surrounded by an imaginary bubble that constantly changes shape and size depending on certain conditions. It extends everywhere around the planet and is full of energy created by the life force of humans, animals and flora and fauna. It's called a morphic field.

Humans are very powerful, especially when collectively thinking. They can create and do create change. In fact, the human race is a product of its collective thinking, so there is no need to blame anybody other than ourselves for the way things are. Things are what they are because of our collective thinking, which means they won't change until we collectively decide to change them. It's all down to us — as a collective. We have the power necessary to change things — we can think negatively about each other, and if the thought is strong enough, we create war, which is happening right now, but we can change this by thinking positively. Depending on the number of people collectively thinking about the same thing at the same time, we can change things straight away, so let's do it!

A carefully controlled scientific demonstration of collective thinking and meditation was carried out between June 7 and July 30, 1993. The study involved a coherent group of people; they increased in number from eight hundred to a maximum of four thousand over the trial.

A week or so after the start of the study, violent crime, homicides, rapes and aggravated assaults, measured by the FBI {Uniform Crime Statistics}, began decreasing, and continued to drop until the end of the experiment.

Before the project, the researchers had publicly predicted that the coherence group would reduce crime by twenty per cent. This prediction had been ridiculed by the Chief of Police who asserted that the only thing that would decrease crime that much would be twenty inches of snow. In the end, the maximum decrease was 23.3 per cent. This significant reduction occurred when the size of the group was at its largest in the final week of the project, and during a blistering heat wave! When the project disbanded, crime began to rise again.

This is proof that collective thinking can and does affect an outcome! Doctors sometimes give placebos to patients for different reasons; often the patient gets better, which means unknowingly, they have cured themselves… the point here is that we are much stronger than we think.

Years ago, I decided to start a business in Cairns in the tourist industry. I was building a horse drawn wagon to be used to take tourists around the inner city. Unknown to me, at the same time another person was building a wagon in Manly, Sydney. We both opened our businesses, almost at the same time within two weeks of each other. One of us, or both of us, had picked up the idea unintentionally from the morphic field. This meant that both of us had been working on similar projects for about a year.

This is often why people think of an idea to go into business, then someone else does exactly the same thing in a completely different part of the country. When an idea comes to you, you can be sure that if you don't act on it someone else will. This is what I mean when I talk about the invisible bubble around the planet… there are also smaller bubbles or morphic fields around countries, and smaller ones around cities, and if you go really small, there are fields around individual humans and animals!

You have probably all had this experience when someone is introduced to you for the first time, you pick up a sense at the time of the introduction. The closer you get to the person the stronger the feeling is, because in a sense you are entering into the bubble that surrounds them, and likewise they are entering into yours. Some of these bubbles that people have around them are so big that you can sense them the instant they walk into a room. These people with exceptionally big bubbles can sometimes be important people, but mostly they only think they are — they have a big 'ego'. This can be okay if you like the person, you can feel at ease and comfortable in that situation.

On the other side of the coin, you sometimes meet a person and the closer you get, the more uncomfortable you feel. This is a two-way street by the way, as they can, depending on how sensitive they are, feel uncomfortable as well — a sign to be wary… It's a warning, and if you don't heed it you can easily end up on the wrong track again. For example, one day we were having a BBQ; it was a sunny day and most of the guests had already arrived, but one couple were late. I'd started the cooking but suddenly felt exhausted; I knew that the late guests were very near because I was picking up the woman's severe depression she often suffered with. About five minutes later they walked in all smiles, but for me there was no hiding how she was feeling.

I know you all have probably had this feeling that I'm talking about at one time or another, but often we are in a situation where we have to push on anyhow, simply because of a work situation for example. But as I said, the spirit or our personal guide is always trying to help us, even if we aren't listening most of the time.

Chapter 27

Another reminder — you are the spirit not the body, the body is just the vehicle the spirit chooses to get about in. When the spirit chooses a human body to be with or use, it has a general plan — it wants to experience certain things in this lifetime on Earth. It communicates to the body through the right brain, that's where we get our hunches and feelings from. The type of feelings I am talking about is impromptu advice that often doesn't make much sense to us as there usually is no logic to it.

Okay, let's imagine for a moment we are driving down the freeway, the logical thing is to keep driving at the same speed, because it is a good road and there are no obstacles in front of us that we can see. Because the spirit is in control of everything, it sees much further down the freeway! It sees a big pile up, so it says to the physical body steering the vehicle, "Slow down, slow down." The little voice keeps saying it, and if we listen and slow down it may seem illogical but could save our lives! However, most of us normally choose to go with the logical directions of the left brain because it appears to make more sense. This is because the left brain and physical body can only see a short distance — it all looks safe on the freeway, but it doesn't see the pile up two or three kilometres ahead.

The spirit can see everything and knows what will or will not happen down the track in life and can therefore give you the correct advice. It is very difficult for the spirit or soul to get its own way, because as humans, we are brought up with material values and hardly any spiritual values or understanding.

There is more that is unseen than seen. When we look outside, we can see the sky and the ground, while in between there might be trees and houses that we can see in the distance, but that's the limit of what we see. If you're a bird looking straight down from a high vantage point, you would see much more of the picture, and from a different angle. What we see in the first place is not all there is, in other words we see very little of what there **really** is.

I have heard people say, "believe only what you see and half of what you hear." Of course, that's nonsense. Take electricity for example — you can't see it, but you know it's there because you can feel it if you touch a live wire.

In the physical world we see only a tiny sliver of reality. There are trillions upon trillions of planets yet unknown; we can't see them even with our sophisticated telescopes, but they are there.

Radio waves are flashing through the air all the time to our mobile phones, to our TVs, to our radios, and if we could see them all, we would be ducking the whole time for fear they would hit us! In fact, there are numerous other things going on around us that we are totally unaware of, because we don't have the senses to see them. The spirit or the soul is also invisible to us, but to most sensible people, they realise it exists.

Humans are stuck in the material way of thinking; most people think if you can't see a thing it doesn't exist. Every living creature on the planet has a spirit, and if you could see the spirits, you would find that they are everywhere, as are all physical beings. In a sense there are two worlds living side by side simultaneously — the physical and the nonphysical. {You could say the earth and its parallel, everything has a double, like positive and negative, darkness and light.}

We can see the physical with our eyes but there are many more things that we don't see. Take electricity again — we all know it's there, we use it all the time, it is strong and powerful and is everywhere, but we can't see it. The energy from the spirit world, which is the driving force for all our existence, surrounds us all the time, but again we don't see it and so some people even doubt that it exists.

The spirit has to communicate with the physical body that it's controlling. It does this through giving us what we call feelings or hunches. When you meet somebody for the first time, you sometimes get a strong feeling about that person, it may be a warning from your higher self to be careful, or maybe just to relax and feel comfortable. Sometimes you might be about to do something, suddenly you may get a feeling of caution, or even extreme caution; it's so strong sometimes that you just stop what you're doing. This is because the spirit can see the big picture, whereas our physical bodies can only see what is physically in front of us. We must try and cultivate this asset as it is imperative to our spiritual growth and well-being.

Another example — when sailing on a yacht at sea level, you can only see as far as the horizon. The rest of the picture that is over the horizon is out of view, but the island that you may be heading for is still there. If you were in an aeroplane, for example, you could look down and see the yacht and also see the island just like the spirit; the view is far greater so it's just a matter of one's perspective.

The physical body only sees a small part of what's about to happen in life, but the spirit can see everything. This is why it is so important to listen and take notice of those little warnings that you get from your spirit. Remember, it is always trying to help us, all we have to do is listen and take notice — it's that easy. Animals listen and take notice all the time because it's natural and normal to them, but we humans struggle on, using only our left logical brain.

The material values that we treasure, including getting a good job, buying a house, making sure our children are in the correct school etc. etc. are only part of the dialogue in the play, which can create conflict between the spirit and our physical desires. The spirit tries to steer its host body one way, while our material body with its material values and lack of spiritual understanding, tries to lead us in another direction.

We are taught what's right and wrong through our childhood, and on into our adulthood. We are told that material gains will at the very least, make us well-off and secure, and at the end of the day will make us all 'happy'. I'm sure you have all thought, 'when I get my new car, I will be happy', or 'when I get my new house, I will be happy', or 'when I get a raise in my salary, I will be happy'. And on and on it goes.

Most of us realise after a while that these material gains only make us 'happy' for a **very** short time, and so we think we might need more of the same to fix the problem — on and on we go continually seeking the same thing. We are always trying to satisfy our cravings, but craving for what? That's a good question… I can think of many rich people who haven't figured this simple lesson out, and so they continue to try and get even **more** money, in the belief that one day enough money will fix their cravings! It's a bit like giving an alcoholic a glass of water and saying to him, "this will satisfy you," but of course it won't. Until we realise that we are using the wrong 'fix', we could spend many lifetimes chasing our tails and spiritually treading water!

Chapter 28

There are many other types of false fulfilment, for example seeking positions of power in the belief that this will do the trick. Many people want to be leaders, whether it be in the workplace, or leading a country, but at the end of the day nothing works. Rich people often don't know when to stop, and powerful people in positions of leadership, don't know when to stop either. History has shown us that after a while, being a leader of one country isn't enough, so they try to conquer other countries, but it still doesn't satisfy; enough is never enough for these people.

Most of the serious issues on this planet are caused by power seekers, or financial greed seekers, in their efforts to fill their emptiness. Until they realise that the emptiness is a deficiency in their spiritual diet, they haven't got a chance. The human race is constantly trying to satisfy its spiritual diet but being materialistic and living in a material world without spiritual values, we only see a material answer to fulfil our emptiness.

The way to get spiritual fulfilment starts by taking the

advice and direction given to you by your spirit/soul that sees all — this means giving over to it and simply 'trusting' it. Until we get this part of our lives in order, we are all going to stay on the merry-go-round, and things on this planet will only get worse.

Recently, more and more people are realising that they are in desperate need to satisfy their emptiness; as a result, they go to greater lengths in their desire to become satisfied. Examples of this can be seen everywhere: there is more and more drug use, world leaders intoxicated by power, religious leaders that would like to take over the world for their self-gratification, dare devil stunts like bungee jumping. Whatever it is, it never seems to be enough, and we just demand more and more and go to greater lengths in our search.

More and more greed, more and bigger wars, it's all becoming extreme — even the planet is becoming extreme with its weather patterns. Of course, you can call it global warming, and there is always a logical reason (left brain). I believe the spiritual connection is the most important thing in our lives.

Something has to be done and soon! The human race is reaching a decisive peak and we have to realise we are all looking in the wrong place for our answers. We must all start looking at our spiritual values and live our lives in a totally different way.

When a person becomes spiritually fulfilled, they have no desire for great material gains or power, or the need to be liked or looked up to. If the human race would only realise that their existence here is just temporary, they would then realise that gaining material things is of no real value, other than to provide shelter and food for the physical body. I'm not saying here that having a nice car and a nice home are not important, but they are really just life's little comforts in the play.

The most important thing is our spiritual development, that after all is the only thing we can take with us, so that has to be our main or only real objective. What seems important is only important until we forget it, and then it's nothing — until we remember it again. In other words, the problems that seem so big, often don't even materialise — hence they are not a problem, only a fear of a possibility which may never happen. If we trusted, we would find life considerably easier.

Chapter 29

As an analogy... the journey through life is like walking on an escalator at an airport in the wrong direction; we feel we have come a great distance in our sixty or seventy years of life, but one only needs to look at the advertisements on the wall to see that we haven't moved at all. The sense of movement is there, but it's an illusion.

As I have said before, time moves around — ask any child waiting for Christmas, and compare their year with their parents, where Christmas seems to come all too quickly. Our concept of time is inaccurate, time moves around considerably for everybody and everything. In fact, in the big picture, everything is happening now, even though there are different things happening at the same time, which gives us the feeling of some sort of movement which we refer to as a passage of time. Try to imagine that every page in the great book has already been written and each page is transparent. We now can look through the book without turning any pages... We do not move along, we just see anything and everything at the same moment because it is all now.

There is a lot we don't understand, but we have to remember that everything is now, rather than being in the past or future. The theory we have about this material world is incorrect from a spirit world point of view.

There is also clearly something going on with what we call time. Another thing that is unusual, is the physical way we see things, we see things as we are programmed to see them.

When a baby is born it has a fixed program, to a degree. The first thing it does is to take a breath of air, even though no one has taught it to do that. The second thing it almost always does is cry, because it may be hungry — this is called instinct. These programs are fixed, as is the way we see things on this planet. What this tells us is things here aren't necessarily as we perceive they are!

This view applies to time as well. Take a fly, for example, that lives only a few days — we think that's a very short time, but for the fly it's a full life. This is a good example of the values in measuring what we call time. If things on this planet aren't necessarily the way we view them, and this includes time and colour, and probably numerous other things that I haven't touched on, then what exactly is this place really like? I keep coming back to the fact that this is just a play, and we are seeing all the backdrops and props as the 'producer' has designed us to see them. We are privileged to be asked to act in this greatest of plays.

Enjoy your journey!